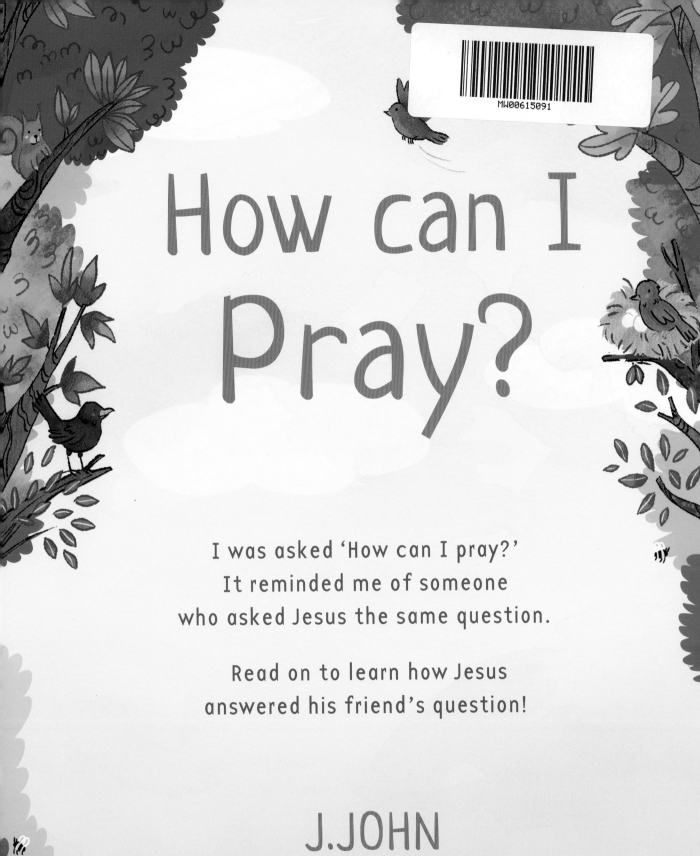

How can I Pray?

I was asked 'How can I pray?'
It reminded me of someone
who asked Jesus the same question.

Read on to learn how Jesus
answered his friend's question!

J.JOHN

Illustrated by Morena Forza

About praying

God created the world and everything in it – including us!
People have always talked to God through prayer.

We use prayer to thank God, praise God and ask God to help us in times of need.

But there are always questions.

Who are we praying to?

God showed himself in Jesus and he promised that whoever followed him would be able to know God too. Jesus taught his followers how to pray.

Jesus told his followers,
'Pray like this.'

Our Father in heaven,

    may your name always be kept holy.

May your kingdom come

and what you want be done,

    here on earth as it is in heaven.

Give us the food we need for each day.

Forgive us for our sins,

    just as we have forgiven those who sinned against us.

And do not cause us to be tempted,

but save us from the Evil One.

The kingdom, the power and the glory are yours forever.

Amen.

This is what's called the *Lord's Prayer* and you can find it
in the Bible in Matthew's gospel, chapter 6, verses 9-13.

Many people just repeat this prayer – and I pray it every day – but actually it's a *pattern* for how to pray.

Think of a colouring book full of black and white outline drawings for you to colour in as you want.

This prayer is a bit like that.

Let's look together at the Lord's Prayer...

Our Father

When people write letters they begin with the name
of the person they are writing to, like 'Dear John'.

You might expect Jesus to say that when we pray
we should start 'Dear God' but instead he told
his friends that they could begin 'Dear Father
in heaven'.

If you believe in Jesus you can become his friend.

Friends of Jesus can call the
God of the universe 'Father'.

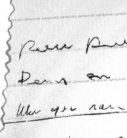

God is the perfect parent
and he loves you very much.

In heaven

Jesus said that God is our Father in heaven.
In heaven there is nothing bad or sad,
and everything is perfect, good and happy.

And remember, even though God is running
the whole universe, he wants to hear from you.

May your name always be kept holy

No one is happy when they hear people treating their name in a bad way. Being rude about someone's name is being rude about them.

Because God is perfect, it's wrong to treat him or his name without being kind or respectful. When we pray we need to treat God seriously and with respect.

He is our Father in heaven but he is also mighty and holy.

May your kingdom come

When we let God be our king and Jesus our friend then God's kingdom spreads out a little further from heaven.

God has promised that one day his kingdom will spread everywhere so that absolutely everything that is bad and sad will stop forever.

And because God's kingdom is full of love, joy and peace, we pray that this will happen soon.

When we pray these words, it also means that we want to work with God to help make his kingdom come.

What you want be done, here on earth as it is in heaven

To do what God wants means
telling the truth, being kind to people
and not doing mean and nasty things.
We don't just need to be friends with Jesus,
we need to be kind and good as he was.

The reason why God's kingdom is so wonderful and
happy is because everybody in it does what God wants.
So we are to pray that this whole world will be like
heaven and obey God and follow Jesus.

Of course, if we pray this we
are saying that we are going
to try to do what God wants.

Give us the food we need for each day

When we pray, it's good to put God first and *then* we can pray for ourselves.

So now we can ask God for what we need. Because everything we eat is a gift from God, it's good to ask him to give us food. That's why I say, 'Thank you, God!' before I eat my meals.

Actually, this prayer is not just about food; it's about asking God for *everything* we need to live, such as being kept safe and well.

And forgive us for our sins

What do you think should be done about people who do wrong things to others?

Like most people, you probably think that they should be stopped and made to pay for what they've done wrong.

The trouble is, we all do lots of wrong things to God all the time. But Jesus says we can ask God to forgive us for what we've done wrong, and if we really mean we are sorry and we promise not to do it again, then God will forgive us because he loves us.

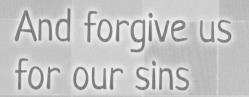

To be forgiven by God means that the wrong things we have done can be made clean, like when we have had a bath after playing in the mud in the garden – the dirt washes away.

Just as we have forgiven those who sinned against us

God forgives the friends of Jesus who admit what they've done wrong and ask to be forgiven.

That is something to be really happy about.

But if God forgives us, we should be like him and forgive other people.

So if someone has done or said something that has hurt us, we shouldn't try to hurt them back. This is what adults call 'taking revenge'. Instead we should forgive them.

Sadly, though, some people do things that are so bad it's important we tell other people, such as teachers or parents, so they can make things right.

And do not cause us to be tempted

Temptation is when we feel that we want to do or say something wrong – like stealing, lying or being rude or unkind. Jesus doesn't want his friends to give in when they are tempted to do bad things.

It's very difficult to do the right thing instead of the wrong thing, so we need to pray and ask God to help us.

The secret to not giving in to temptation is to stay close to Jesus.

But save us from the Evil One

God doesn't want us to do wrong things but the Bible tells us that there is someone who does want us to do them. Jesus calls him the 'Evil One'.

He's nowhere near as powerful as Jesus but he wants to make us do, say and think what is wrong.

Let's pray for Jesus to help protect us.

The kingdom, the power, and the glory are yours forever

When we have finished praying it's good to end by thanking God for who he is.

To praise God is to remind ourselves that he is the true King of the universe, that he is bigger than all our problems and that, one day, the whole world will truly be his.

Praising God helps us feel excited and encouraged after praying. It reminds us that however difficult things may seem to be, God – our Father in heaven – is in charge of everything and that because Jesus is our friend we can always go to him for help.

Amen!

Amen is a little word. It's like when you are writing a letter, you read it through carefully and then finally put your signature at the bottom. If you do that it means that you agree with everything you have written.

To say *Amen* at the end of a prayer means, 'Please, God, make what I've prayed happen.'

When should we pray?

I pray the Lord's Prayer every day – it is the first prayer I pray when I wake up in the morning.

I encourage you to do the same and pray when you have problems...

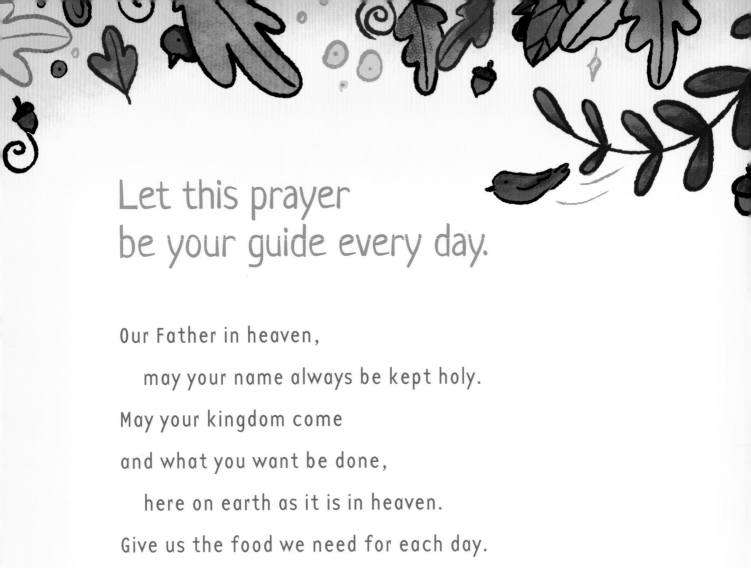

Let this prayer
be your guide every day.

Our Father in heaven,

    may your name always be kept holy.

May your kingdom come

and what you want be done,

    here on earth as it is in heaven.

Give us the food we need for each day.

Forgive us for our sins,

    just as we have forgiven those who sinned against us.

And do not cause us to be tempted,

but save us from the Evil One.

The kingdom, the power and the glory are yours forever.

Amen.